Let's TaCo 'BOUt the BiBLe

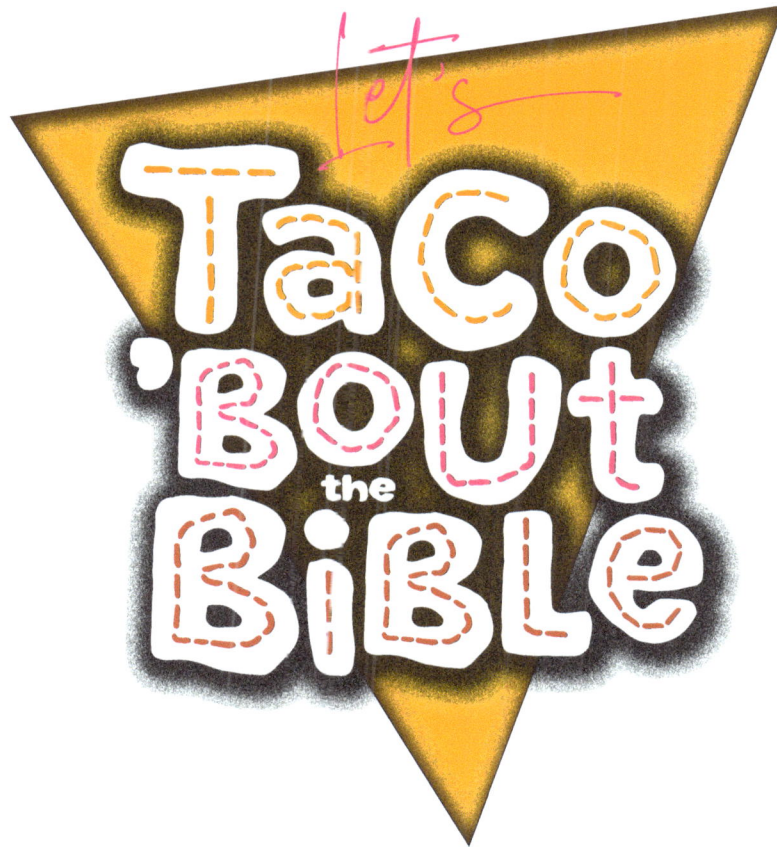

with **Timmy T.** *and* **The Spicy Little Numbers**

WRITTEN & DESIGNED BY BRIAN KAUSTE

PARENTS: May this help ignite a passion for God's Word in your kids
and may He continue to give you all you need as you champion your child's faith adventure!

LET'S TACO 'BOUT THE BIBLE

© 2025 Kaunsept

WRITTEN & DESIGNED BY BRIAN KAUSTE

ISBN: 978-1-4866-2687-8
eBook ISBN: 978-1-4866-2688-5

Word Alive Press
119 De Baets Street Winnipeg, MB R2J 3R9
www.wordalivepress.ca

WORD ALIVE
—PRESS—

Cataloguing in Publication information can be obtained from Library and Archives Canada.

This book
BELONGS TO:

_____

Hi! I'm Timmy T.

You probably guessed I'm a taco! I'm CRUNCHY on the outside, but full of good stuff on the inside. Did you know that I **love** to read? It's true! And guess what? My favourite book is...

...the Bible!

It's a really, really BIG BOOK and can be hard to understand.

The **good news** is that my friends and I are here to help! Wanna

meet them? Ok, turn the page. Let me introduce you to...

The Spicy Little Numbers!

These are NACHO ordinary little chips. While I like things mild, they love things spicy. They also love **numbers**. How high can you count? That's great! Looks like you're ready, so...

3 2

4

5 1

...let's begin!

How many **numbers** do you see? Yup - there's five! Each Spicy
Little Number will use one of them to tell you about the Bible.

They're super EXCITED, so let's get things going with...

1 story

Did you know the Bible is actually ONE BIG STORY?

It's God's story, filled with lots of great stuff He wants to tell us!

Here are a few more **interesting things** to know about the Bible:

it has
66
books

it has over
40
writers

it was written in
3
languages

it took over
1500
years to write

One more thing! The story of the Bible can be split in four ways:

1 **creation**
(yay!)

2 **fall**
(boo!)

3 **redemption**
(double yay!)

4 **restoration**
(infinity yay!)

You can think of the Bible as a library full of many amazing books!

testaments

There are **66** books in the Bible that are split into two parts: the **OLD** Testamant and the **NEW** Testamant. The word testamant means covenant or **PROMISE**. Check it out:

the OLD TESTAMENT has 39 BOOKS

the NEW TESTAMENT has 27 BOOKS

Genesis Exodus Leviticus Numbers Deuteronomy
Joshua Judges Ruth 1 & 2 Samuel 1 & 2 Kings
1 & 2 Chronicles Ezra Nehemiah Esther Job
Psalms Proverbs Ecclesiastes Song of Solomon
Isaiah Jeremiah Lamentations Ezekiel Daniel
Hosea Joel Amos Obadiah Jonah Micah Nahum
Habakkuk Zephaniah Haggai Zechariah Malachi

Matthew Mark Luke John Acts
Romans 1 & 2 Corinthians Galatians
Ephesians Philippians Colossians
1 & 2 Thessalonians 1 & 2 Timothy
Titus Philemon Hebrews James
1 & 2 Peter 1, 2 & 3 John Jude
Revelation

SHHH!! God was silent for 400 years between the two testaments!

3
persons

This one is a bit TRICKY. The Bible is God's story and He's made up of three persons. There's God the **Father**, God the **Son** (that's Jesus), and God the **Holy Spirit**. These are known as the

Trinity!

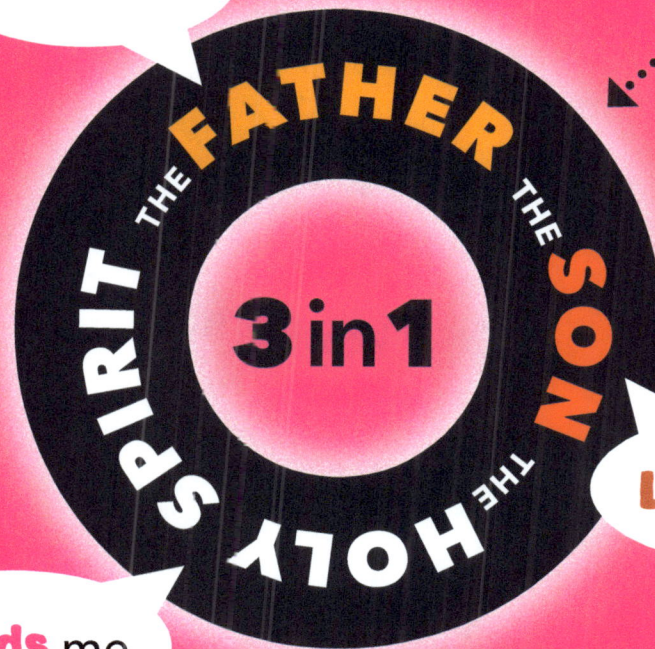

Knows me

Loves me

Leads me

THE FATHER
THE SON
THE HOLY SPIRIT
3 in 1

All three persons were at Jesus' baptism! Check out Matthew 3:16.

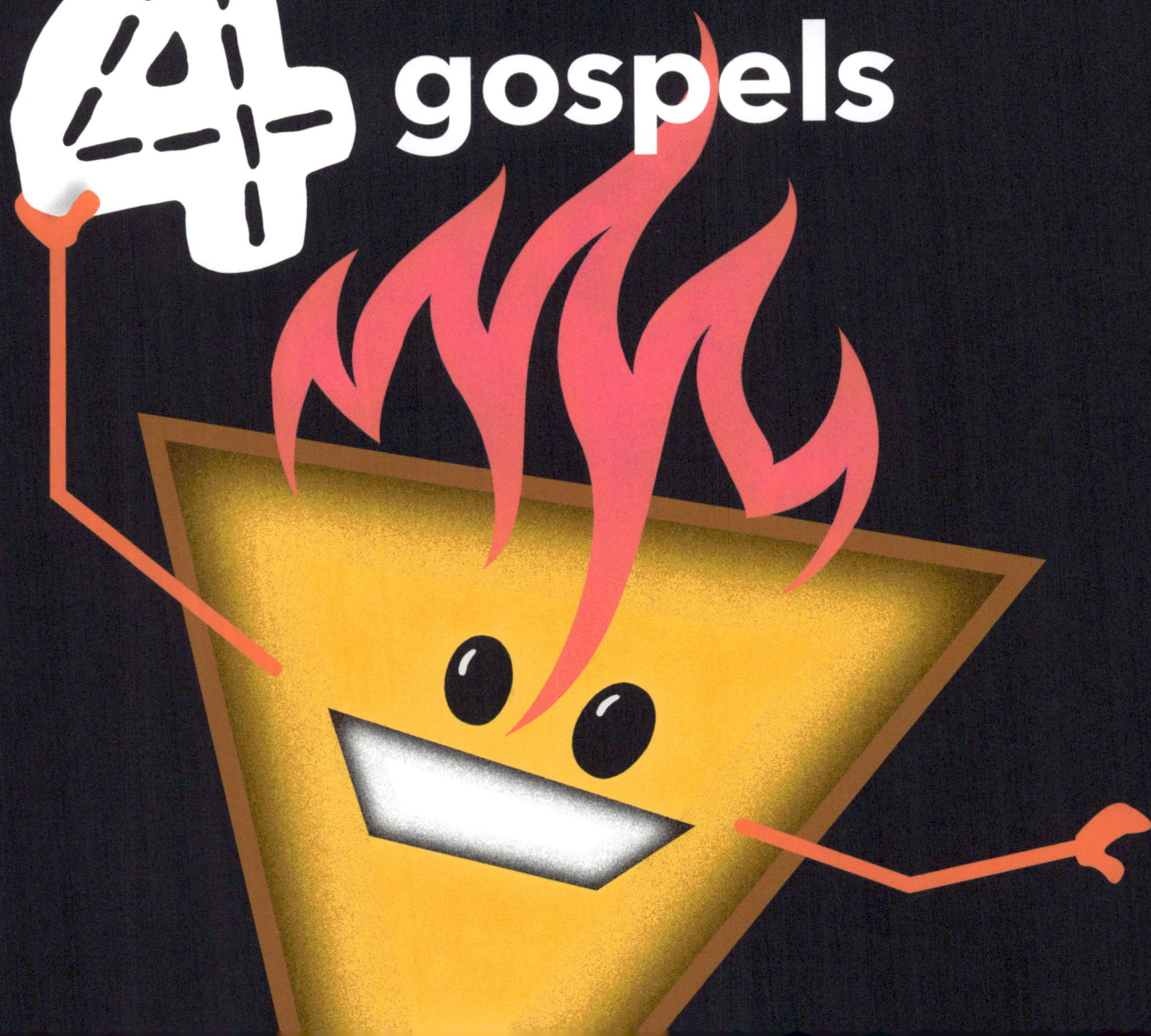
4 gospels

Remember those 27 books of the New Testament? The first four are called **THE GOSPELS**. Gospel means "good news". Here we read about the amazing stories of Jesus and His friends!

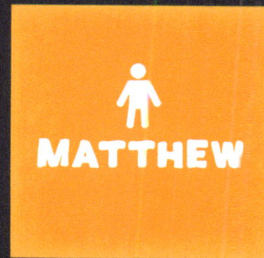

MATTHEW

MARK

LUKE

JOHN

Jesus' friends were called **THE DISCIPLES**. A disciple is someone who follows Jesus. They learned to say the things He said and do the things He did. There were twelve disciples in all!

Why four? It was important to tell the story of Jesus in different ways.

books of law

HIGH FIVE! You made it to the end! **So** much happens in the first five books of the Bible. A guy named Moses wrote them. They were **super** important to the Israelites, who were God's chosen people.

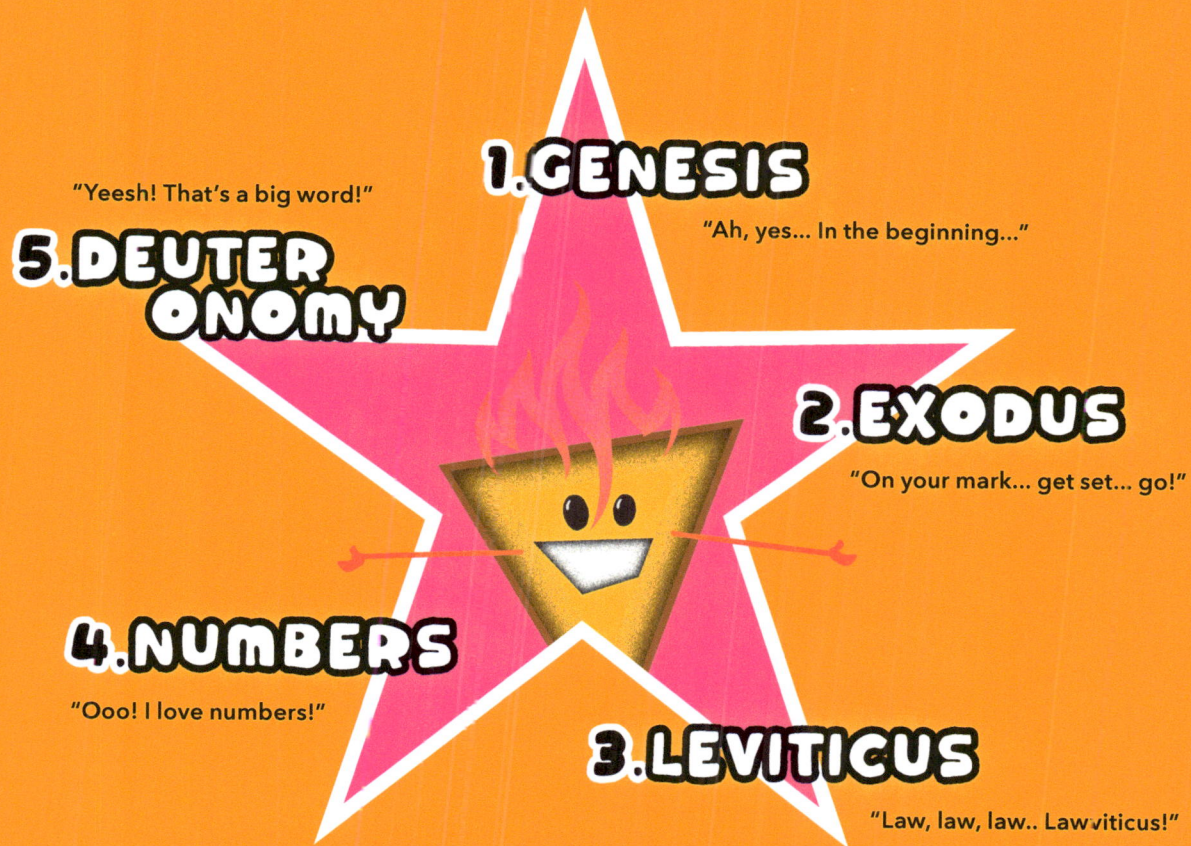

1. GENESIS

"Ah, yes... In the beginning..."

"Yeesh! That's a big word!"

5. DEUTERONOMY

2. EXODUS

"On your mark... get set... go!"

4. NUMBERS

"Ooo! I love numbers!"

3. LEVITICUS

"Law, law, law.. Lawviticus!"

*These books were also known as **The Pentateuch** and **The Torah**!*

Hooray! You did it!

You learned **FIVE** things about the Bible! Remember them all?

You do? That's so great. Let's say them together! **1 Story,
2 Testaments, 3 Persons, 4 Gospels,** and **5 Books of Law**.

Uh-oh, gotta go...

Looks like those Spicy Little Numbers are on the run! There's so much more to learn about the Bible... see ya next time!

www.ingramcontent.com/pod-product-compliance
Lightning Source LLC
Chambersburg PA
CBHW042058040426

42447CB00003B/271